Catphabet

Catphabet

A whimsical celebration of our favourite feline friends

Illustrations by
Meredith Jensen

Harper *by* Design

A is for

(6)

Athletic

B is for

(9)

Bond

C is for

(10)

Charming

D is for

(13)

Devoted

E is for

(15)

Exquisite

F is for

(17)

Friendly

G is for

(19)

Gentle

H is for

(20)

Hairless

I is for

(22)

Imposing

J is for

(25)

Jovial

K is for

(26)

Kooky

L is for

(28)

Legendary

M is for

(31)

Mellow

N is for
32
Noble

O is for
34
Outgoing

P is for
37
Placid

Q is for
38
Quiet

R is for
40
Rescue

S is for
42
Social

T is for
44
Tailless

U is for
47
Unique

V is for
48
Vocal

W is for
50
Woolly

X is for
53
X-Factor

Y is for
54
Young-at-heart

Z is for
57
Zoomies

A is for Athletic

Elite athletes of the cat world, Bengals are a lean, lithe breed that love climbing, running, jumping and adventuring. Not content to sleep the day away, these cunning operators are adept at scaling fences, stealing objects, opening closed doors and patrolling the perimeter of their domains.

B is for
Bond

Birman

Beautiful Birmans love to attach
themselves to their favourite
humans. These precious,
long-haired lovebugs will follow
you from room to room
demanding attention, affection,
cuddles and love, day and night.

C is for
Charming

Scottish Fold

Possessing cute, folded ears and an adorable round face, Scottish Folds charm the pants off everyone they meet. Not one to rule the mean streets, sweet-natured Scottish Folds are happy playing games indoors instead of patrolling the neighbourhood. Known for sitting upright like a human in the 'Buddha' position, you can't help but be charmed when in the presence of a Scottish Fold.

D is for
Devoted

Chartreux

Hailing from France, this uncommon, handsome breed with deep grey fur and amber eyes is a quiet, steadfast companion cat. With a sweet disposition and sharp intellect, this thoughtful feline suits an owner who prefers a drama-free pet. An attachment to a Chartreux will only deepen as the years go by.

E is for
Exquisite

Siberian

With supermodel good looks, the stunning Siberian is perfection personified. Hailing from northern Russia, the Siberian's luxuriously long triple-coat and striking mascara-lined eyes make it a breed that's popular with film and TV-commercial casting agents. While the camera loves Siberians, they're not just a pretty face – this strong, resilient breed has endured for centuries.

F is for
friendly
Burmese

Quick to make friends, the social-butterfly Burmese love watching the world around them, meeting new human friends and, of course, spending time with their family.

G is for Gentle

Ragdoll

These blue-eyed beauties sport a lustrous coat, magnificent bushy tail and distinctive markings. Known for being loving companions that people fall in love with at first sight, the gentle, sweet disposition of the Ragdoll makes them suitable for indoor living, where they'll happily lounge around and nap the day away.

H is for Hairless

Sphynx

Unlike most other cat breeds, the hairless
Sphynx saunters around in all its naked glory.
Prone to sunburn, you'll want to keep these
elfin creatures indoors where they'll enjoy
entertaining you with their silly antics.
When the temperature drops, keep them
warm with a knitted sweater and
they'll love you forever.

I is for Imposing

Maine Coon

Large in stature, with fur-tipped ears and a noble face, the Maine Coon is one of the largest breeds of domestic cat. But don't let their imposing appearance fool you – these cats are actually gentle giants known for making cute chirping and trilling noises. Taking the first part of their name from the state of Maine in the USA, the second half of this breed's moniker is likely due to their bushy, racoon-like tails.

J is for Jovial

Tonkinese

A cross between Burmese and Siamese, the
happy-go-lucky Tonkinese cats adore being around
people so much they're often compared to dogs.
Talkative and playful, these kitties feel at ease
in busy homes filled with adults, children,
other cats and sometimes even canines.
If you want a cheerful cat who
loves having company, invite
a Tonk into your life.

K is for
Kooky

Devon Rex

Consummate clowns, the spirited
Devon Rex loves to play and
entertain. An offbeat breed with
extraterrestrial facial features,
these kitties are known for their
cheeky antics, like swinging
from lampshades and raiding
cupboards. Life is never boring
with a Devon Rex in the house!

L is for
Legendary

Norwegian Forest Cat

The majestic flowing manes and tufted ears and toes of the Norwegian Forest Cats demand attention. Norse myths and legends refer to this large breed as 'fairy cats' or 'troll cats' so its unsurprising that they're strong, active and hardy. While these magnificent beasts are well-adapted to outdoor life, they're also affectionate, making them wonderful companions too.

M is for Mellow

Persian

Forget climbing trees or patrolling the neighbourhood; napping indoors is what Persians do best. This flat-faced, relaxed breed isn't keen on exercising, but is cool with cuddling on the couch, snoozing on a warm lap and other important pursuits that require zero effort.

N is for Noble

Abyssinian

Considered to be one of the oldest cat breeds in the world, many people draw links between the noble Abyssinian and the sacred cats of Ancient Egypt. This fine feline's regal stature and facial features will turn heads, and its sensitive nature, intelligence and loyalty will ensure it is cherished for years to come.

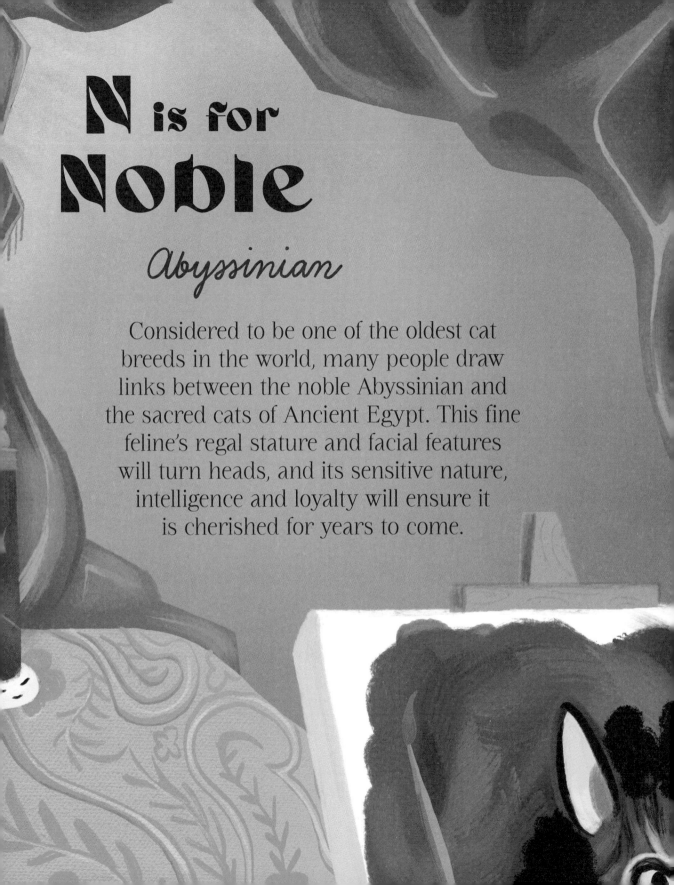

O is for
Outgoing

Turkish Van

Gregarious, friendly and social, the Turkish Van doesn't have time to be aloof. Thought to have originated from the Van Gölü (Lake Van) region of Türkiye, these energetic felines with white bodies and coloured heads and tails aren't backwards about being forward. Fans of playing games and splashing in water, a Turkish Van ensures there's never a dull moment.

P is for
Placid

British Shorthair

A lover, not a fighter, the British Shorthair
is an even-tempered kitty with a stocky
build and a thick, plush coat. While these
round-faced sweethearts are happy
to play, they are also content to
lay back and snooze the
afternoon away.

Q is for Quiet

Himalayan

Some cat breeds need action and adventure, but the magnificent Himalayan prefers more sedentary pursuits like napping on a sunny windowsill or squeezing into an armchair next to a tea-drinking companion. Laidback, calm and with perpetually shocked expressions, these soft kitties are perfect partners for older people and quiet households, where they can luxuriate in peace.

R is for
Rescue

Domestic House Cat

"ROSE"

"WILLOW"

"MAX"

72 cm

60 cm

48 cm

36 cm

24 cm

12 cm

Enduring fixtures of homes all over the world, the ubiquitous Domestic Short- and Medium-hairs are loving companions to cat parents who choose to adopt, not shop. Street-smart, hardy and already down a few lives, mixed-breed moggies like Torties and Tabbies are neighbourhood legends.

"GIZMO"

"HOMER"

"T

S is for Social

Confident and outgoing, these bold little
house panthers love being around people.
Bombays have dog-like personality traits,
so will befriend strangers, visit neighbours
and snuggle up with your other pets.
Keep this active breed busy with toys,
games and plenty of interaction,
and they'll never be bored.

T is for
Tailless

Manx

This ancient breed with its signature
tailless look hails from the windswept
shores of the Isle of Man. Known
for being skilled hunters with
adventurous, playful spirits, the stout
and friendly Manx will adapt to most
situations, experiences and people.

U is for
Unique

Egyptian Mau

One of a few naturally spotty cat breeds, the striking Egyptian Mau is a highly intelligent, agile and trainable feline that comes with a hefty price tag. But what else could you expect from the regal creature that was reportedly revered by Ancient Egyptian rulers?

V is for
Vocal

Siamese

Known for meowing more than other breeds, the Siamese is one chatty catty. Silence is not an option for these lean kitties. Highly intelligent and social, with bright blue eyes, large ears and angular faces, the Siamese will tell you when it's dinnertime, playtime, bedtime ... or any other time for that matter!

W is for Woolly

Selkirk Rex

The curly haired Selkirk Rex turns heads with its unique plush coat reminiscent of a woolly lamb. This cat-in-sheep's-clothing requires regular grooming to maintain its flowing locks, but will reward you for your efforts with plenty of affection and snuggles in return.

X is for X-Factor

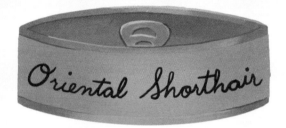

Oriental Shorthair

With a svelte body, long tail, oversized ears and distinctive almond-shaped eyes, the Oriental Shorthair puts the X in X-factor. Whip-smart and inquisitive, these vocal little goblins will steal your heart as they demand your attention, meowing, talking and even honking to whomever will listen.

Y is for Young-at-heart

Snowshoe

A water-loving breed with
distinctive white mittens, the
Snowshoe originated in the USA
in the 1960s and, since then,
has charmed the world with its
fun-loving and affectionate nature.
This somewhat-rare breed's
enduring love of playing with toys
and learning tricks means they
remain young-at-heart well into
their golden years.

Z is for
zoomies

Somali

Not a lazy lap cat, this lively, long-haired relative of the Abyssinian loves to run, climb and jump. Follow its fox-like bushy tail around the house and you'll likely find the Somali getting up to mischief – climbing on perches, tearing up scratching posts, and darting between rooms.

Kitty Club

Abyssinian

Life span: 12 to 16 years

Likes: Climbing and jumping

Dislikes: Being left alone

Bengal

Life span: 12 to 16 years

Likes: Climbing, jumping, playing with water and walking on a leash

Dislikes: Being bored, other cats encroaching on their territory

Birman

Life span: 13 to 15 years

Likes: Spending time with their family and playing games

Dislikes: Being left alone, seeing other pets receive attention

Bombay

Life span: 13 to 16 years

Likes: Playing, climbing, jumping and making new friends

Dislikes: Being bored or confined to small spaces

British Shorthair

Life span: 12 to 15 years

Likes: Napping indoors and quiet spaces

Dislikes: Loud environments

Burmese

Life span: 16 to 20 years

Likes: Climbing, jumping, playing fetch and making new friends

Dislikes: Being ignored or left out of activities

Chartreux

Life span: 11 to 15 years

Likes: Playing with toys, chasing mice and being close to their chosen person

Dislikes: Strangers invading their personal space

Devon Rex

Life span: 14 to 17 years

Likes: Climbing, jumping and learning new tricks

Dislikes: Cold weather and being confined to small spaces

Domestic House Cat

Life span: 15 to 20+ years

Likes: Eating, playing and being close to their adoptive parent

Dislikes: Being distracted from nap time

Egyptian Mau

Life span: 13 to 15 years

Likes: Climbing, jumping, running, learning new tricks and walking on a leash

Dislikes: Cold weather and being left alone

Himalayan

Life span: 10 to 13 years

Likes: Napping indoors and sitting on laps

Dislikes: Hot weather, exercise and loud environments

Maine Coon

Life span: 9 to 14 years

Likes: Making chirping noises, hanging out with humans and chasing mice

Dislikes: Bring separated from their owner

Manx

Life span: 10 to 13 years

Likes: Eating, and chasing mice and insects

Dislikes: Strangers and being separated from their family

Norwegian Forest Cat

Life span: 9 to 14 years

Likes: Going on adventures, chasing mice and patrolling the perimeter

Dislikes: Hot weather

Oriental Shorthair

Life span: 10 to 15 years

Likes: Climbing, jumping and being brushed

Dislikes: Being left alone

Persian

Life span: 10 to 13 years

Likes: Napping, lazing indoors and being admired

Dislikes: Loud environments, small children, hot weather and exercising

Ragdoll

Life span: 11 to 14 years

Likes: Lazing around indoors, sitting on laps, being cuddled and carried around

Dislikes: Closed doors, being left out or separated from their people

Scottish Fold

Life span: 9 to 14 years

Likes: Sitting and sleeping in odd positions

Dislikes: Loud environments

Selkirk Rex

Life span: 12 to 14 years

Likes: Purring loudly, playing with toys and cuddling on laps

Dislikes: Being left alone

Siamese

Life span: 15 to 20 years

Likes: Climbing, jumping and 'singing'

Dislikes: Being left alone

Siberian

Life span: 12 to 15 years

Likes: Playing with water and going on adventures

Dislikes: Hot weather

Snowshoe

Life span: 12 to 15 years

Likes: Being up high, playing with water, and being around children and other pets

Dislikes: Being left alone

Somali

Life span: 9 to 13 years

Likes: Climbing, jumping and playing with toys

Dislikes: Being bored or left alone

Sphynx

Life span: 8 to 14 years

Likes: Running, playing and being close to family

Dislikes: Cold weather and sun exposure

Tonkinese

Life span: 10 to 16 years

Likes: Playing with toys and meowing loudly

Dislikes: Being left alone

Turkish Van

Life span: 13 to 15 years

Likes: Climbing, jumping and swimming

Dislikes: Being bored

Harper *by* Design

An imprint of HarperCollins*Publishers*

HarperCollins*Publishers*
Australia • Brazil • Canada • France • Germany • Holland • India
Italy • Japan • Mexico • New Zealand • Poland • Spain • Sweden
Switzerland • United Kingdom • United States of America

HarperCollins acknowledges the Traditional Custodians of the land upon which we live and work, and pays respect to Elders past and present.

First published on Gadigal Country in Australia in 2024
by HarperCollins*Publishers* Australia Pty Limited
ABN 36 009 913 517
harpercollins.com.au

A catalogue record for this book is available from the National Library of Australia.

ISBN 978 1 4607 6521 0 (hardback)

Publisher: Mark Campbell
Publishing Director: Brigitta Doyle
Editors: Shannon Kelly and Enchinea Close-Brown
Writer: Jo Stewart
Designer: Mietta Yans, HarperCollins Design Studio
Illustrator: Meredith Jensen
Colour reproduction by Splitting Image Colour Studio, Wantirna, Victoria
Printed and bound in China by 1010 Printing

8 7 6 5 4 3 2 1   24 25 26 27